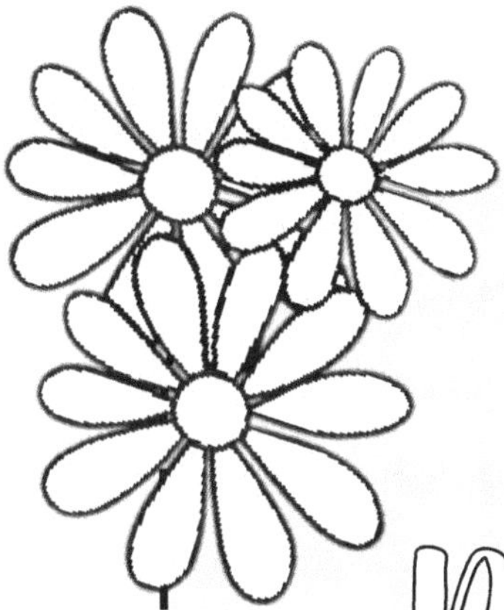

This

Bible Verse

for Girls

Coloring Book

Belongs to:

____

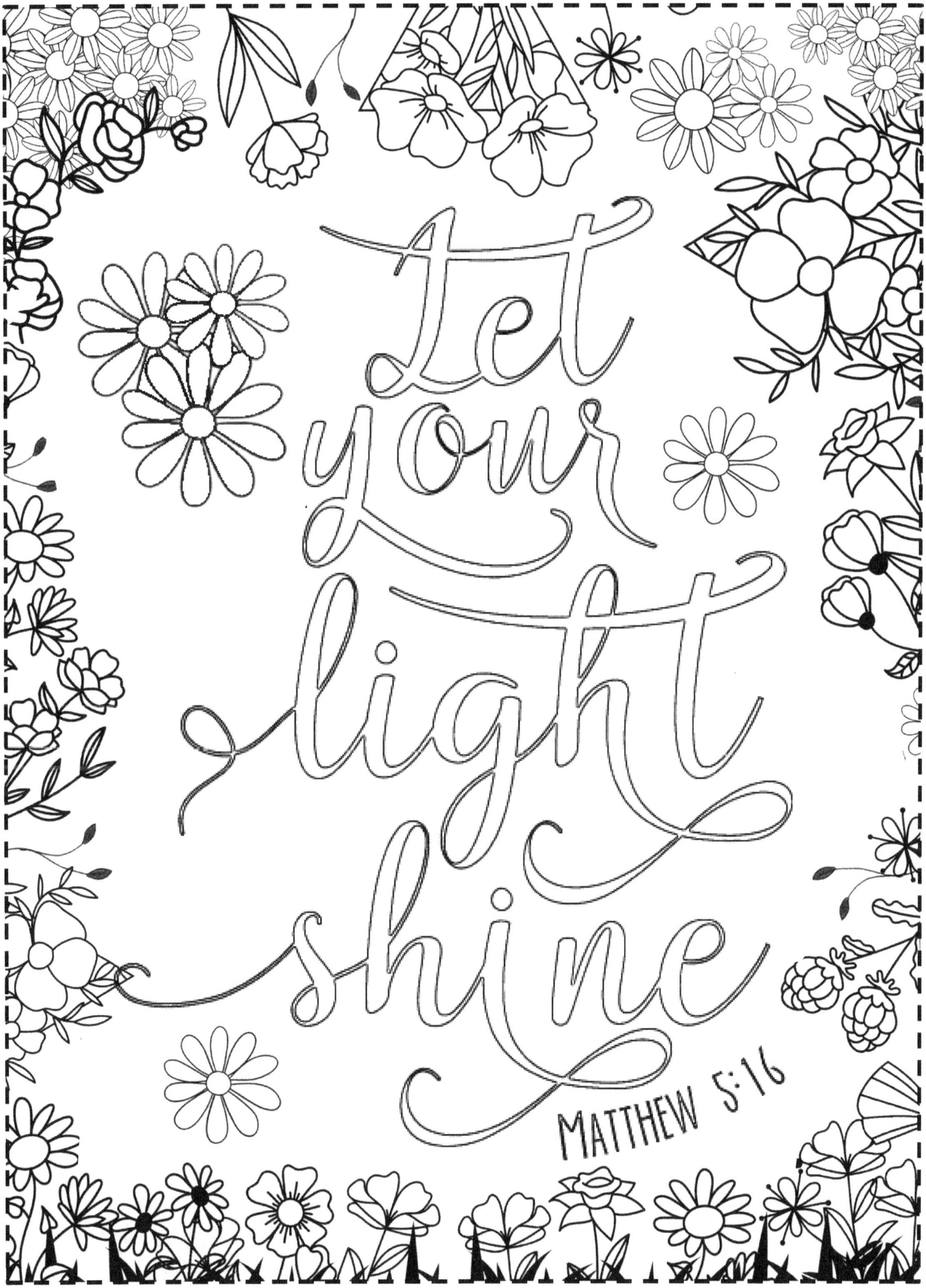
Let your light shine
MATTHEW 5:16

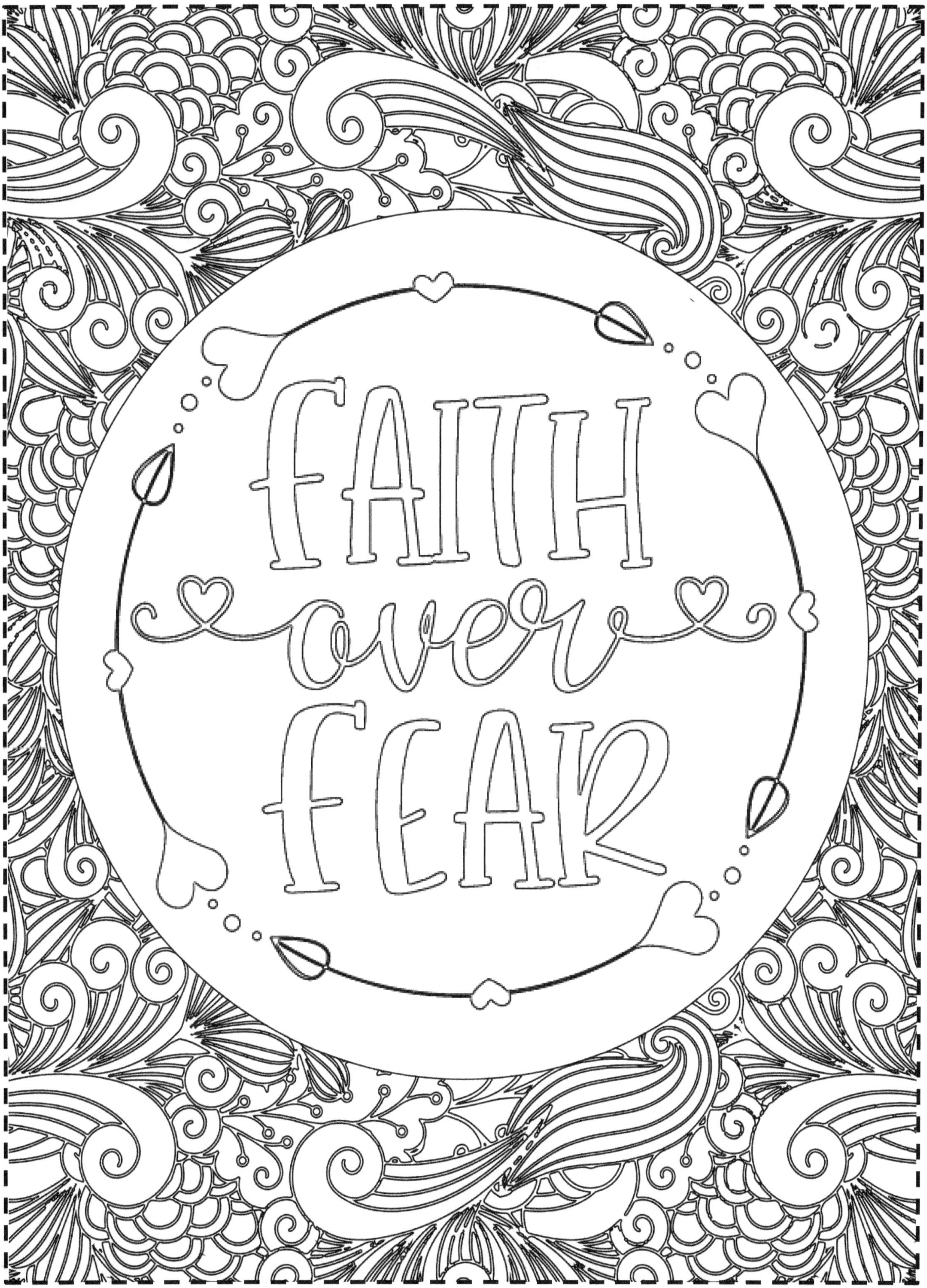
FAITH
over
FEAR

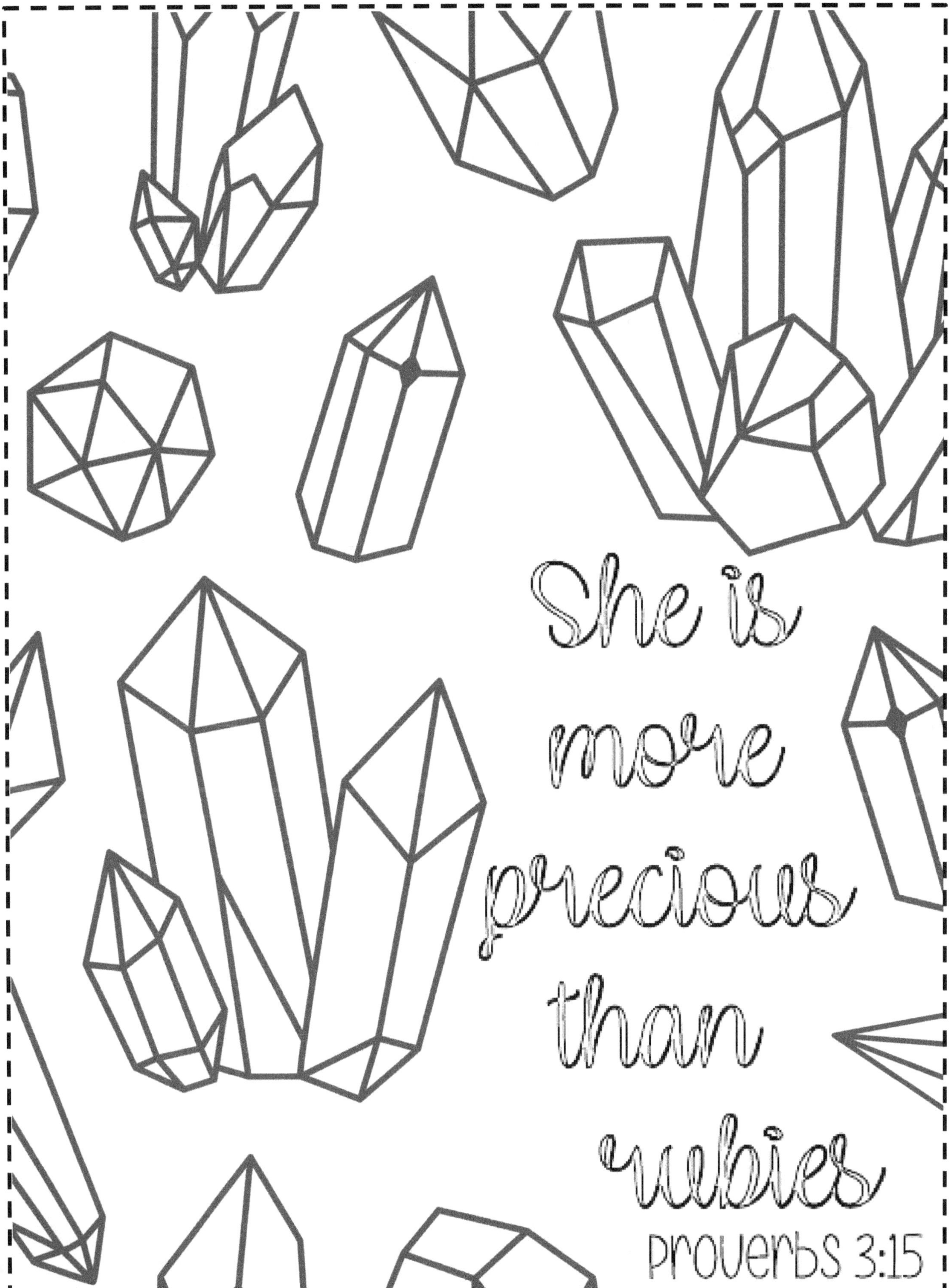
She is
more
precious
than
rubies
Proverbs 3:15

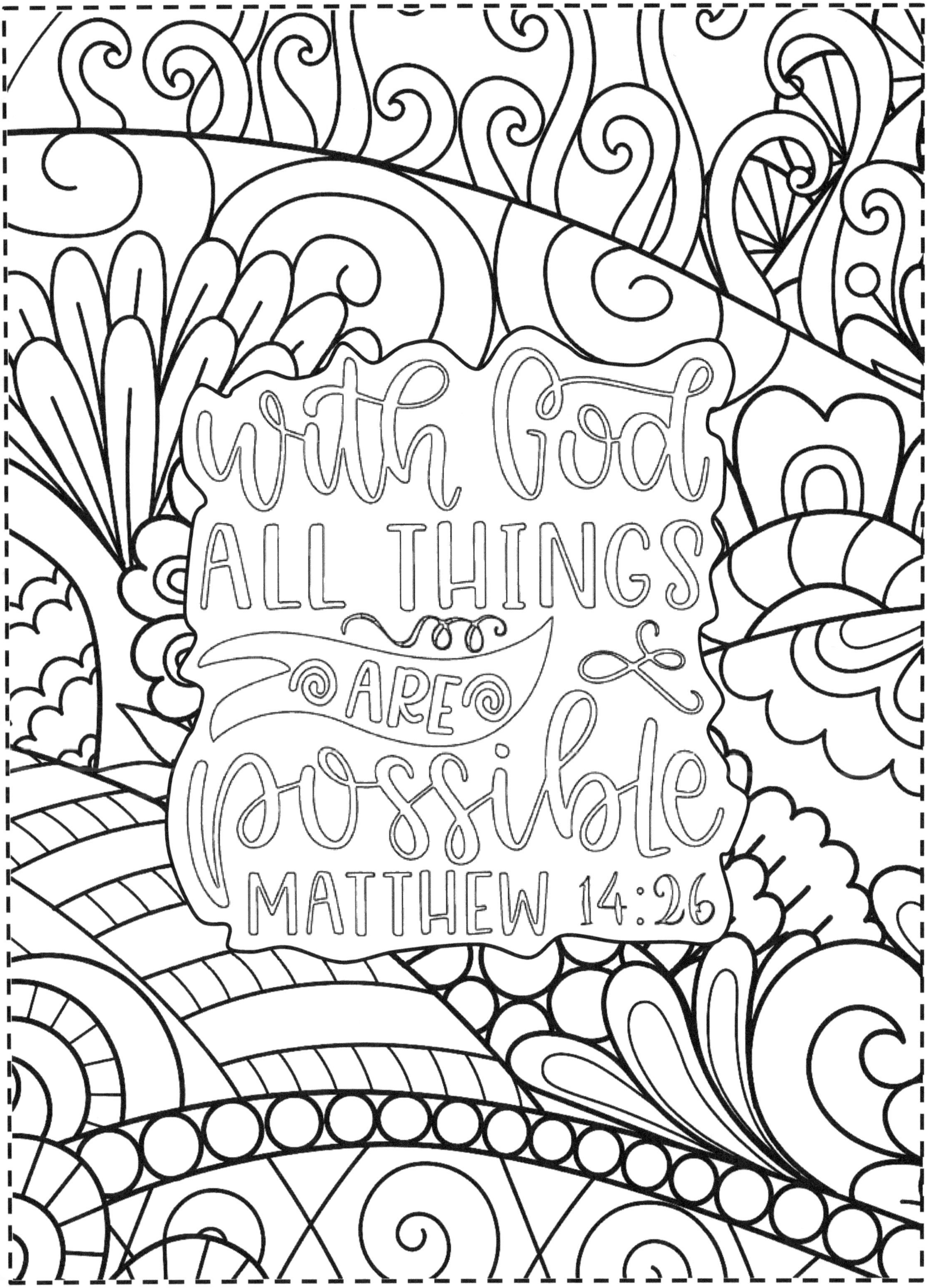
With God
ALL THINGS
ARE
possible
MATTHEW 14:26

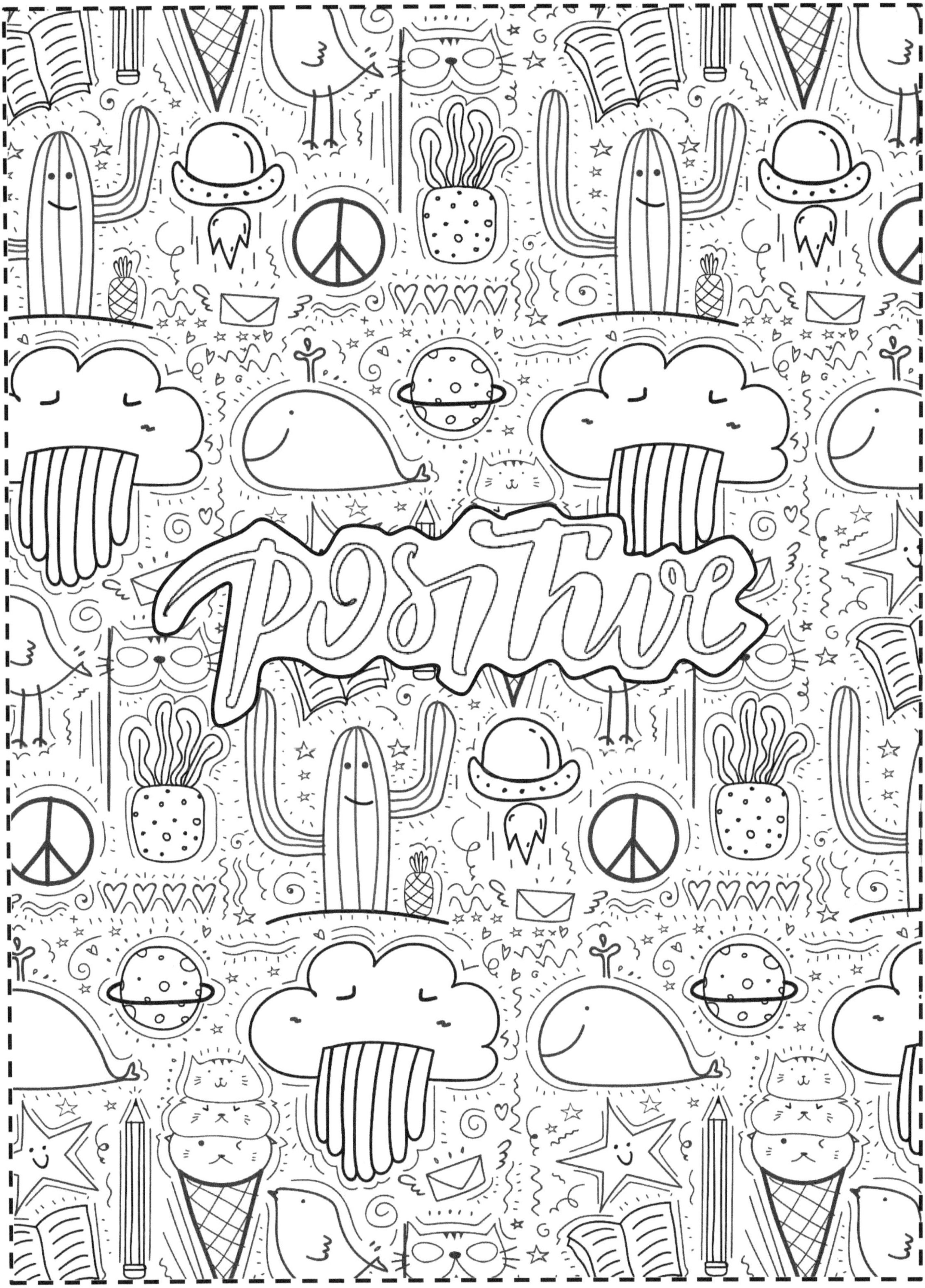
Positive

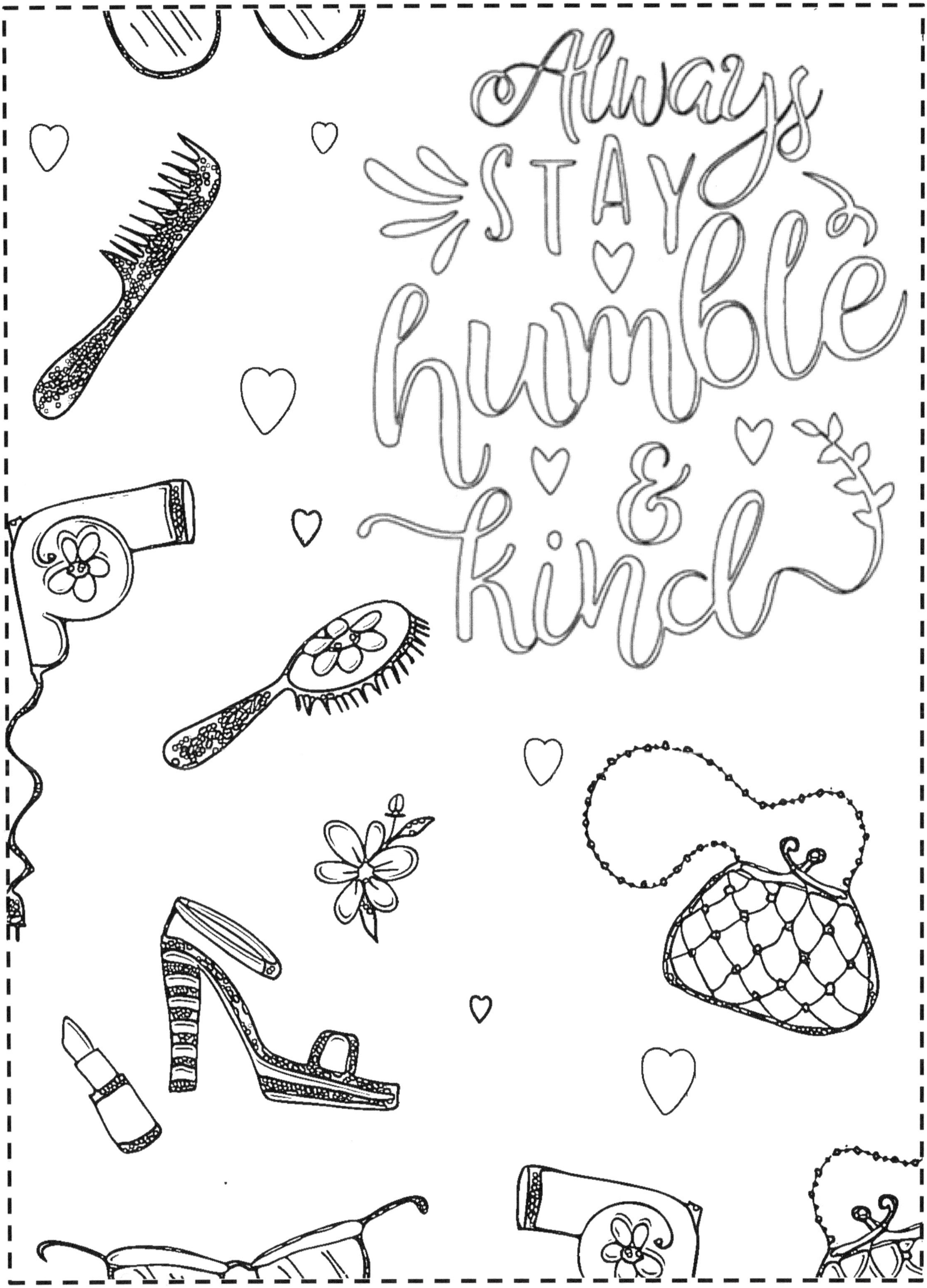
Always
STAY
humble
&
kind

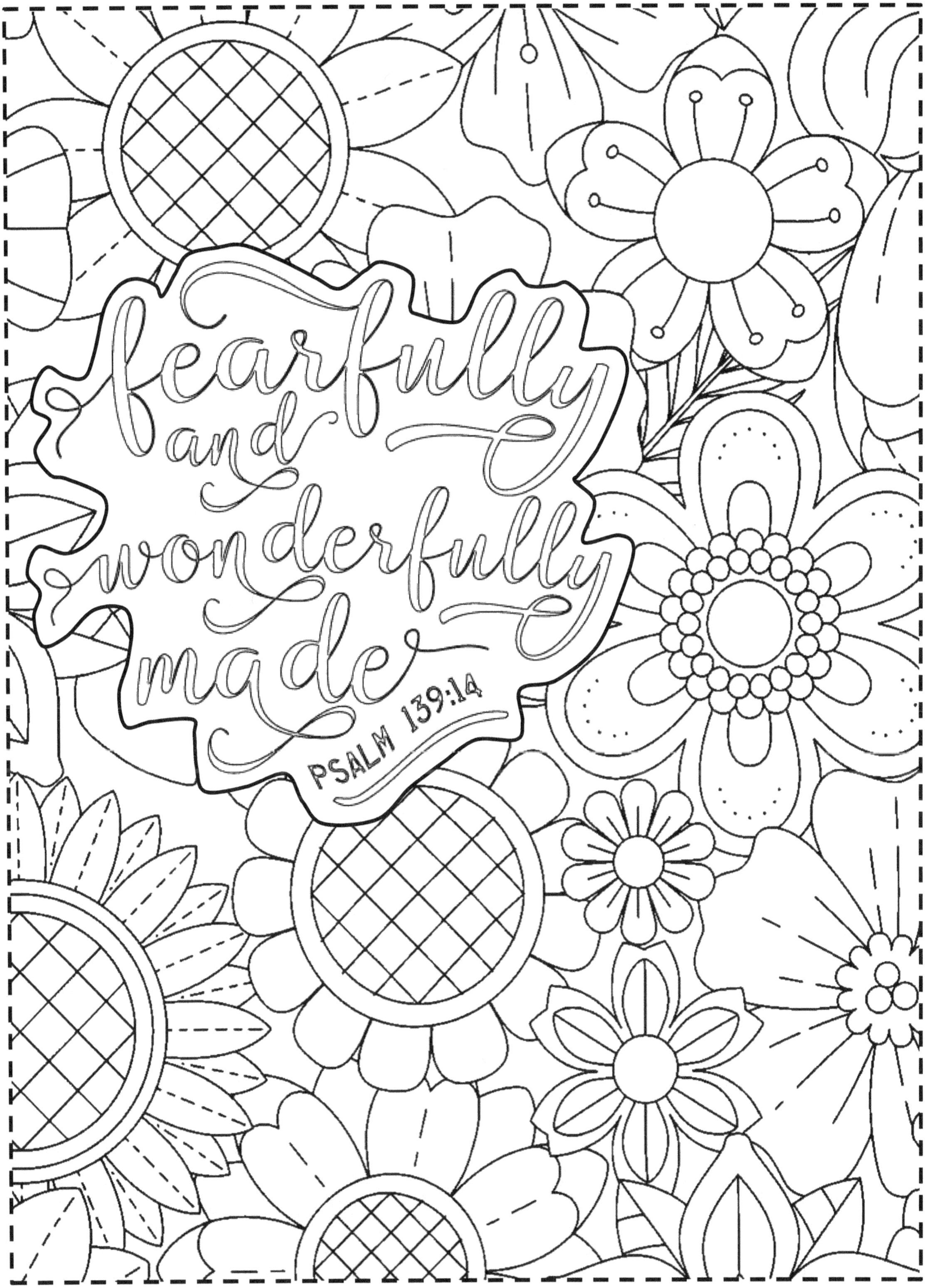
fearfully and wonderfully made
PSALM 139:14

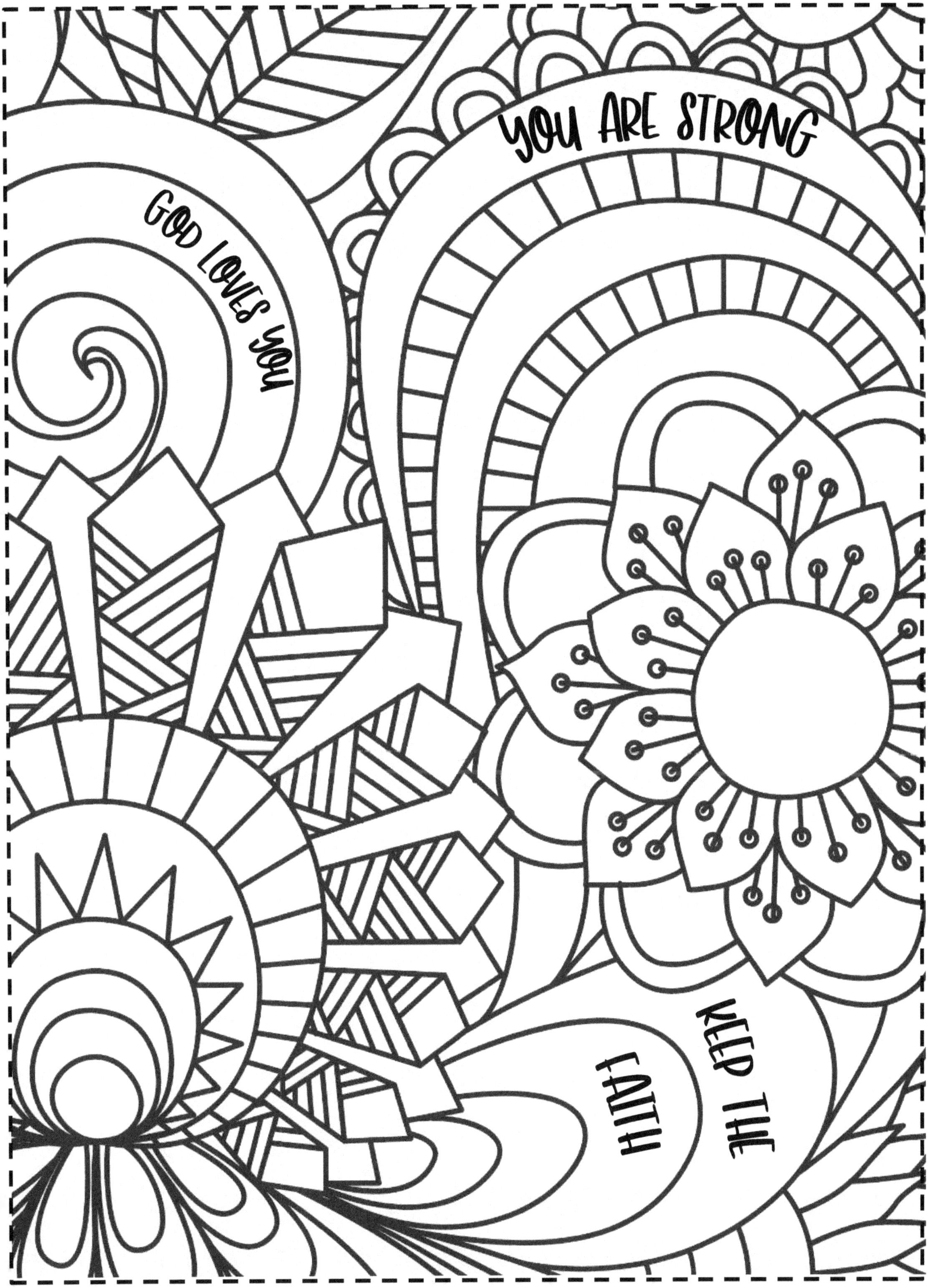

YOU ARE STRONG
GOD LOVES YOU
KEEP THE
FAITH

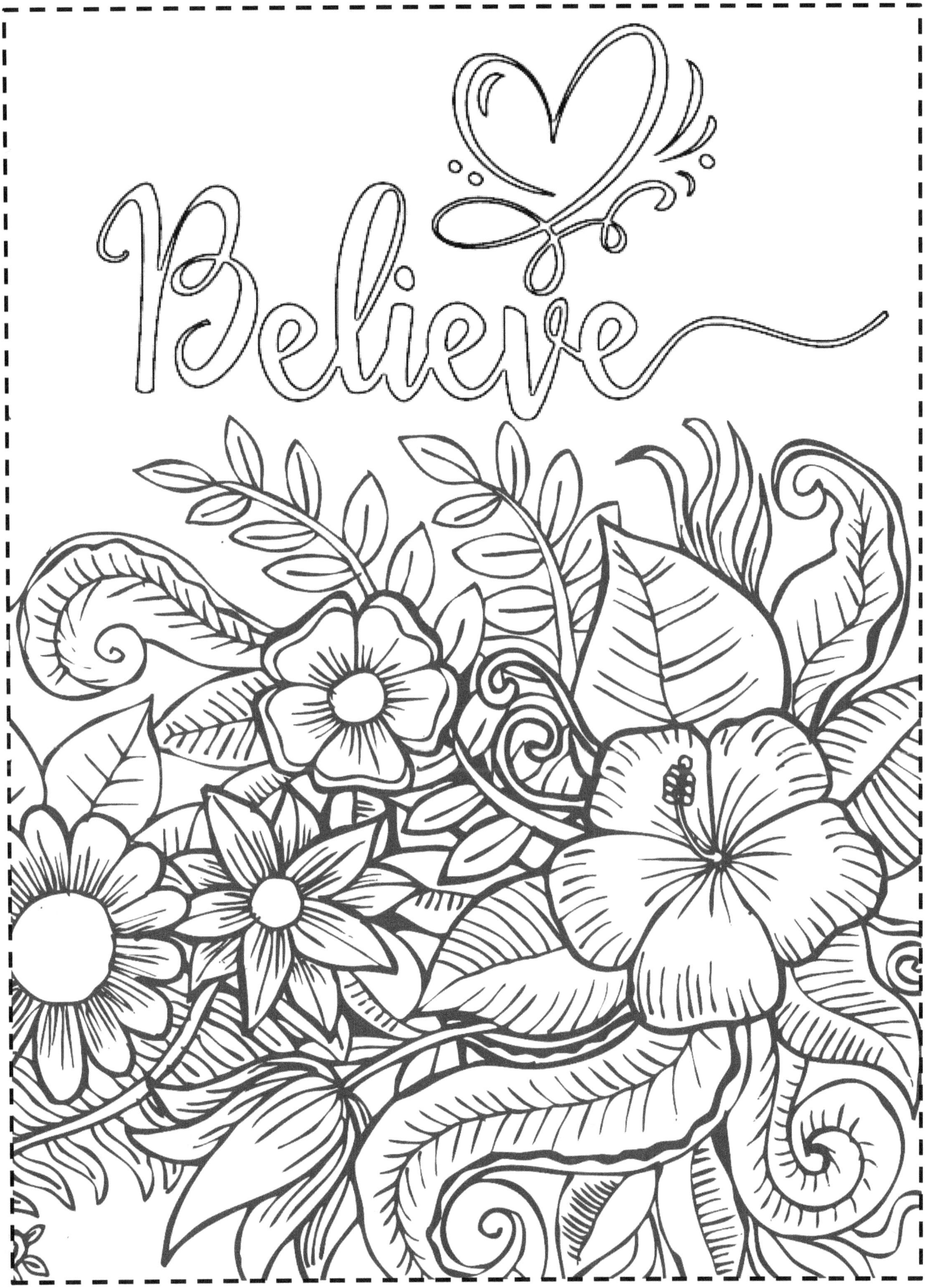
Believe

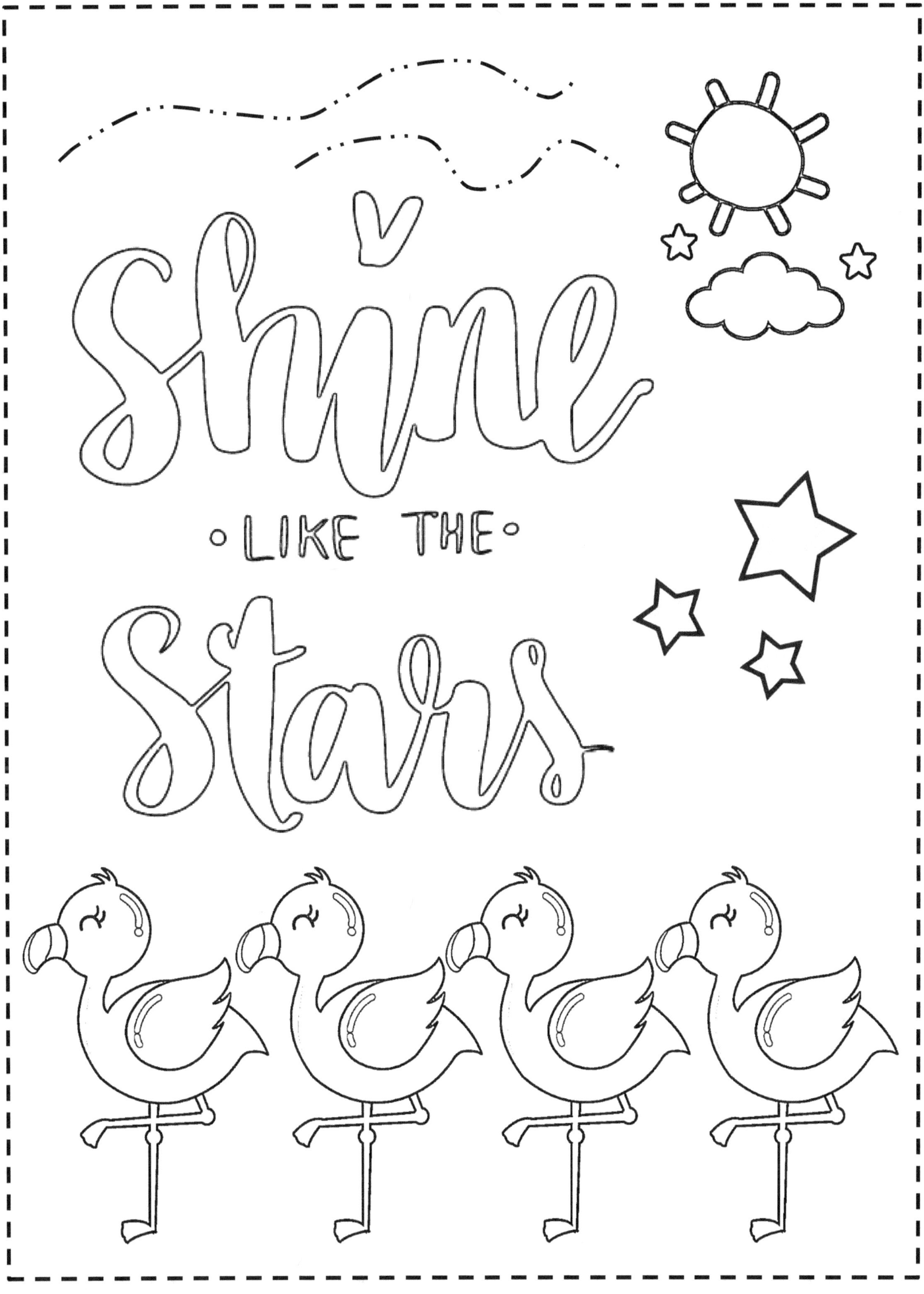
Shine
LIKE THE
Stars

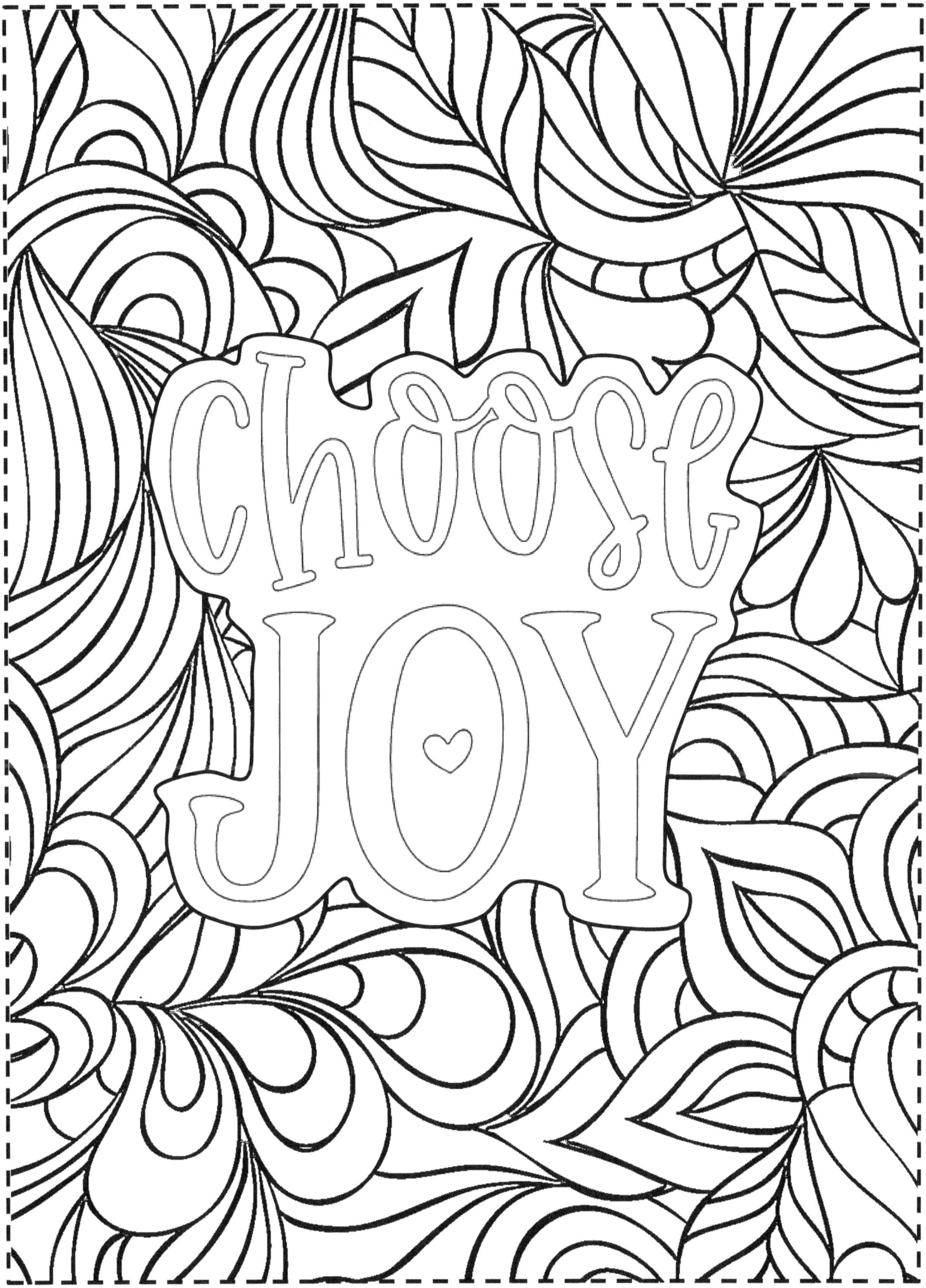
Choose
JOY

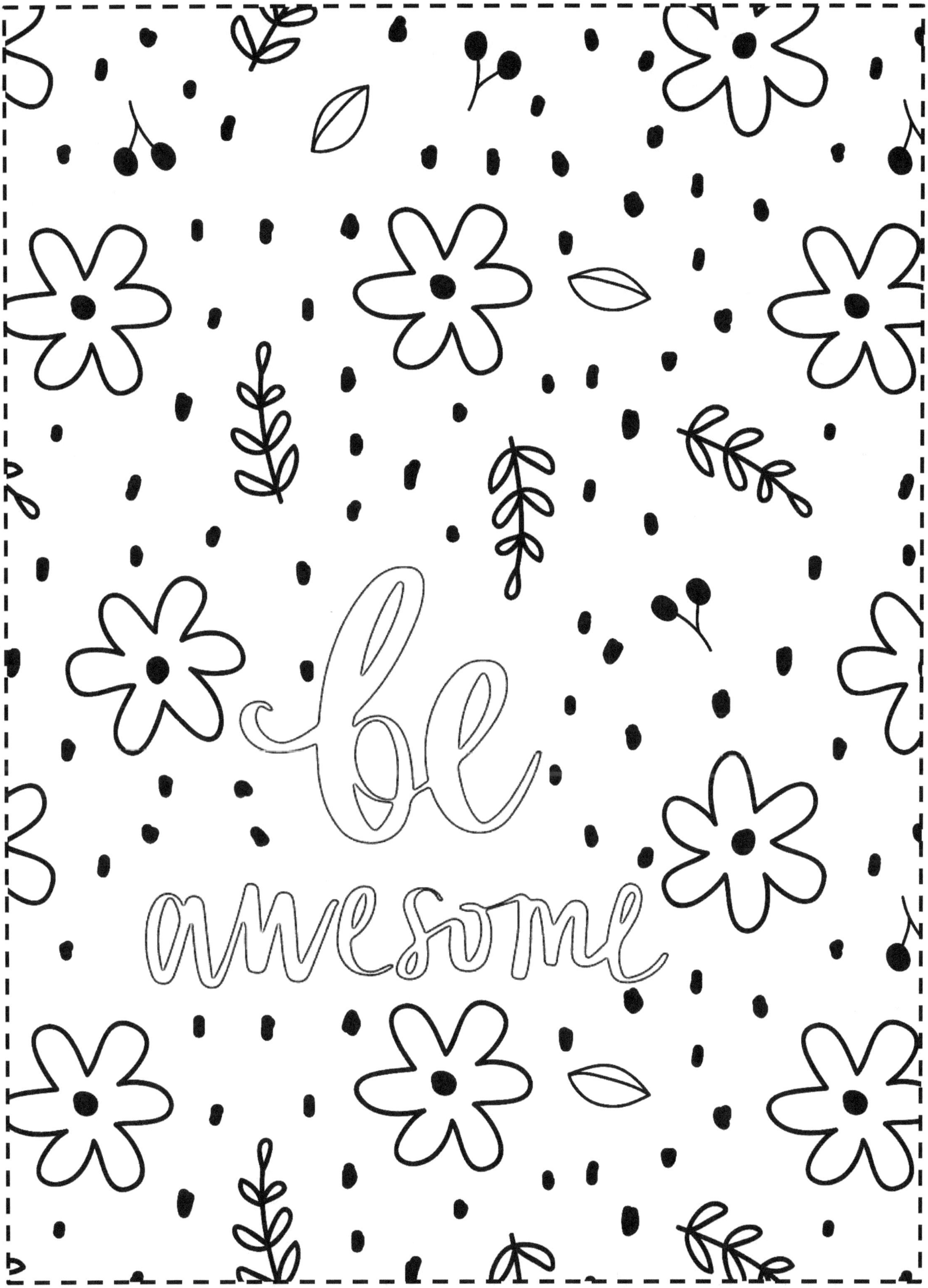
be
awesome

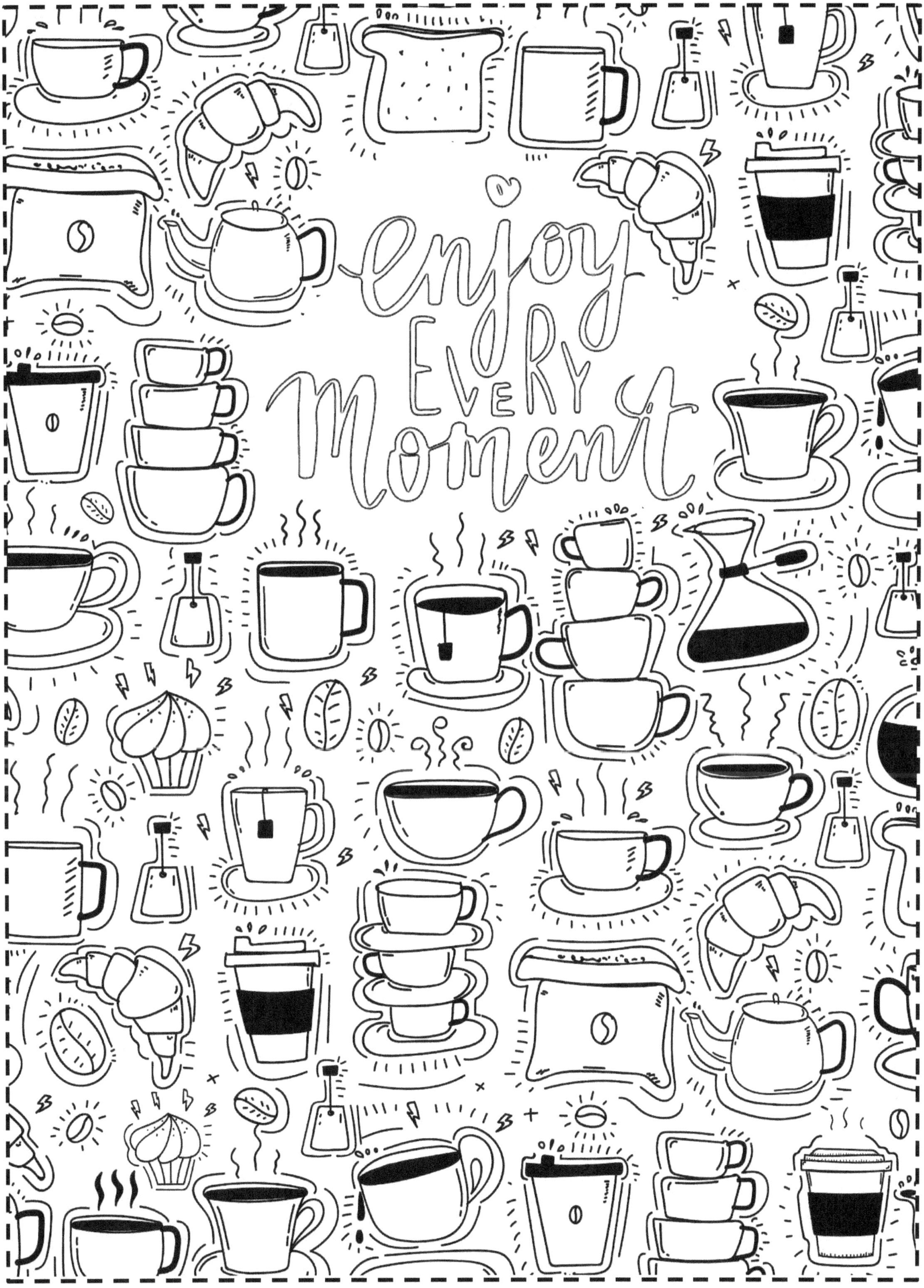
enjoy
EVERY
Moment

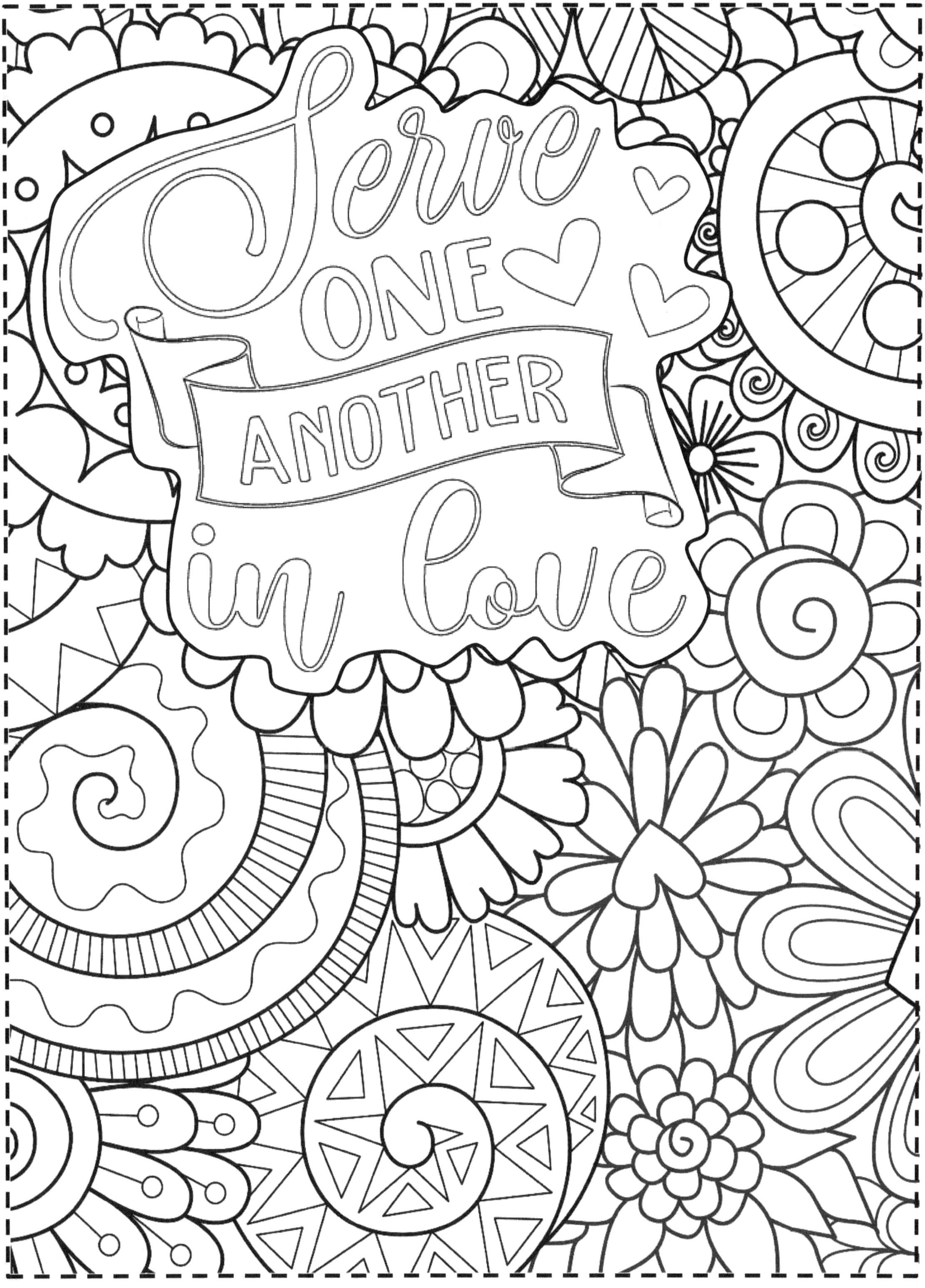
Serve
ONE
ANOTHER
in love

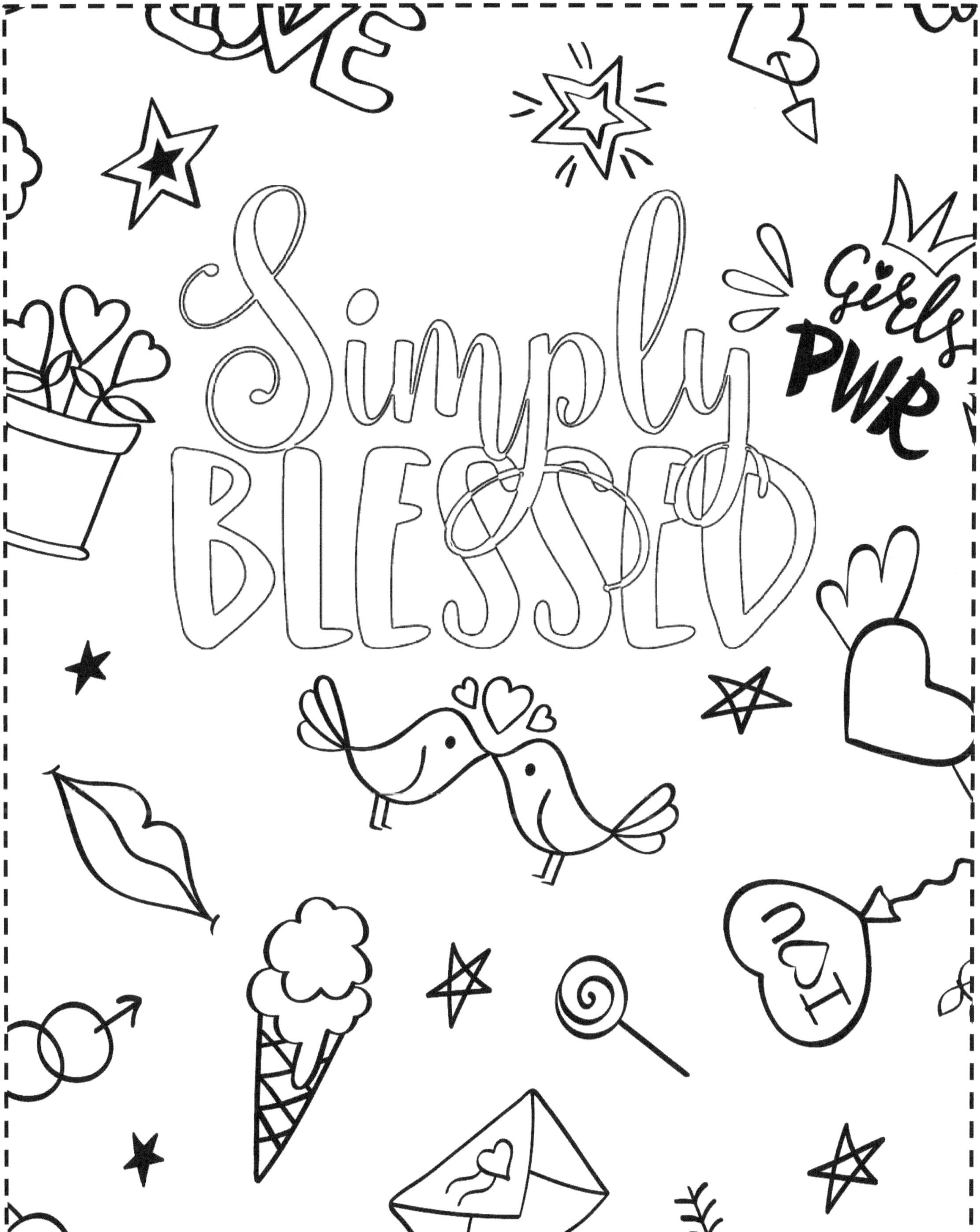
Simply
BLESSED
Girls
PWR
I ♥ U

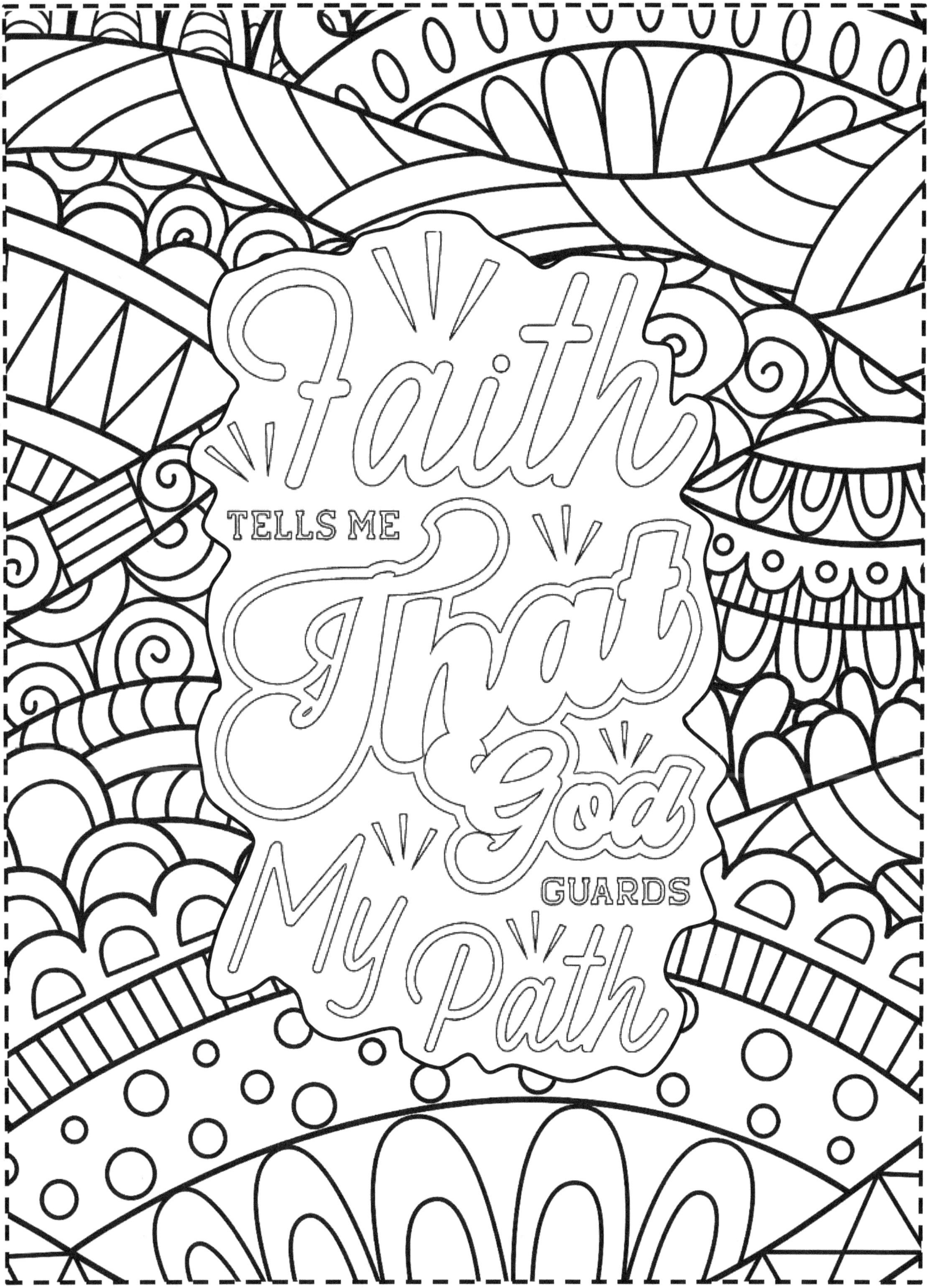
Faith
TELLS ME
That
God
GUARDS
My Path

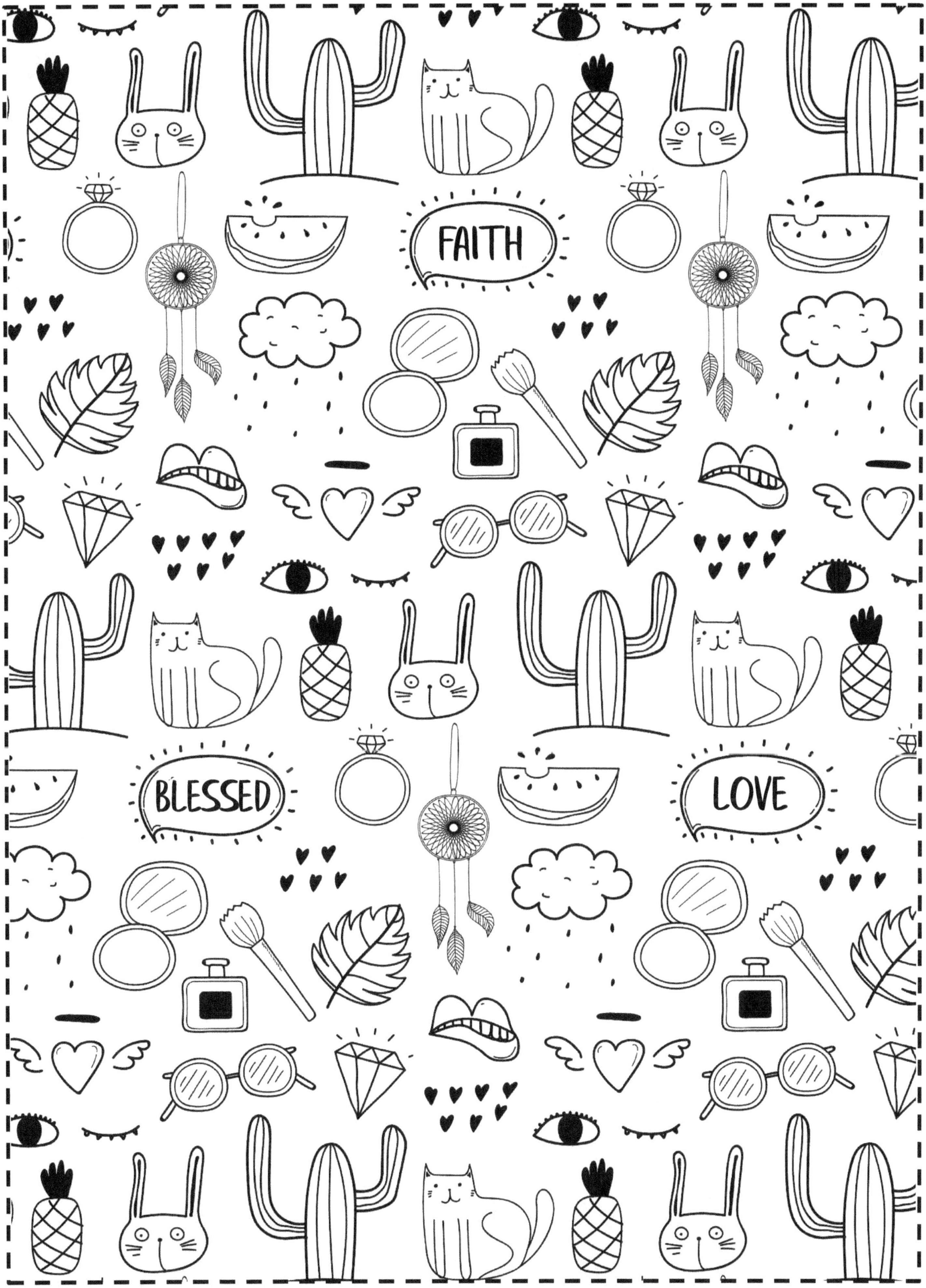
FAITH
BLESSED
LOVE

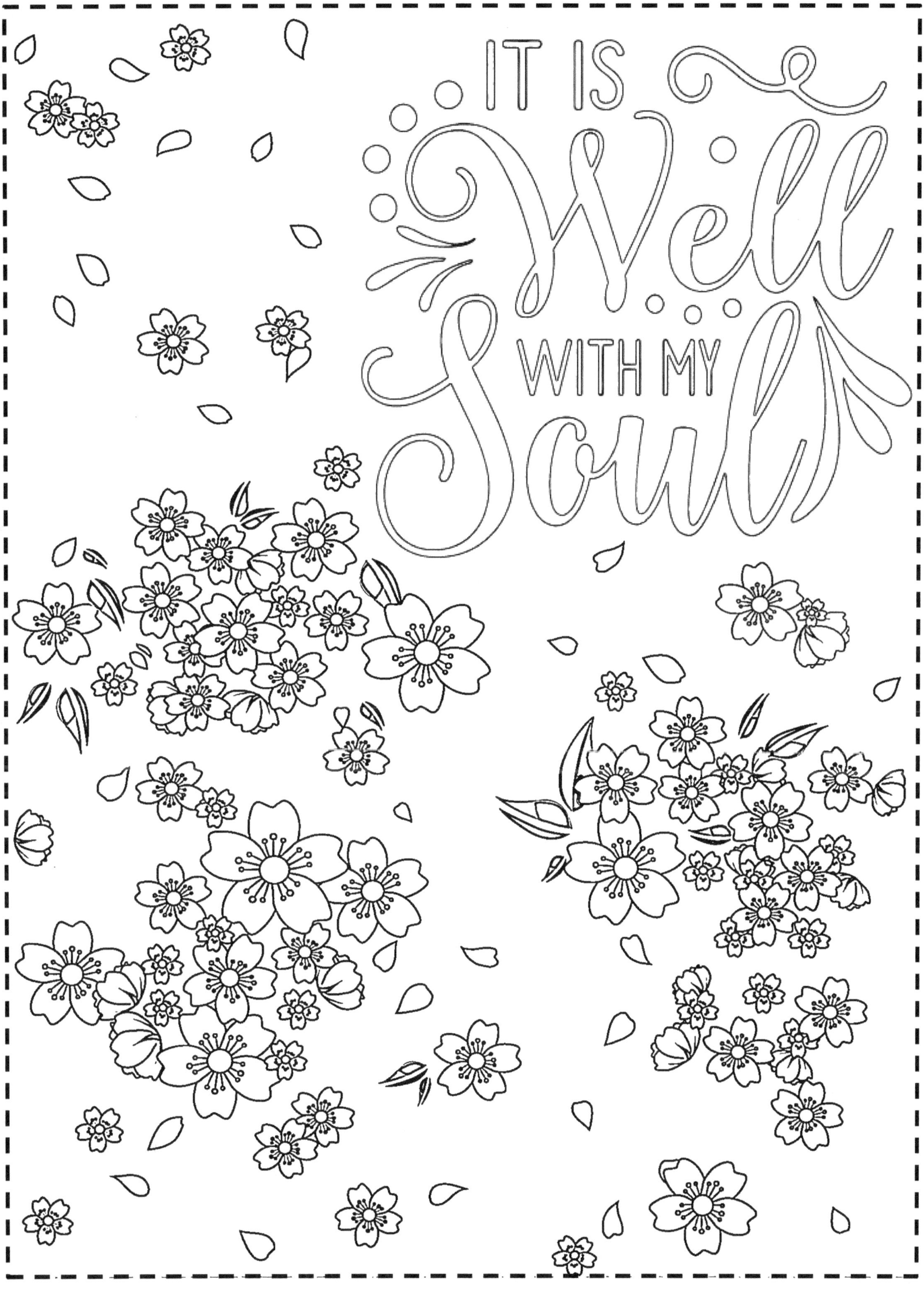
IT IS
Well
WITH MY
Soul

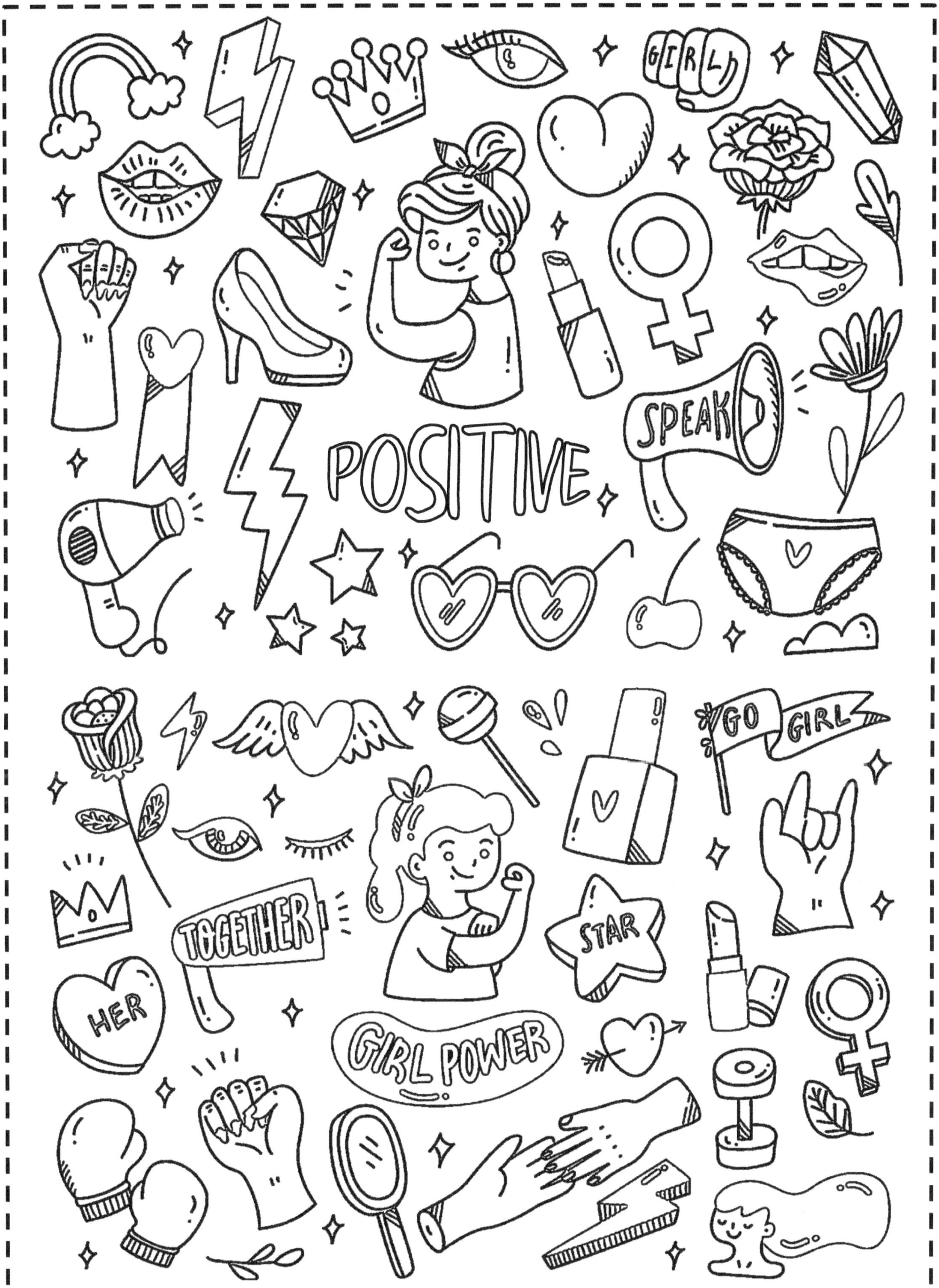
GIRL
POSITIVE
SPEAK
GO GIRL
TOGETHER
STAR
HER
GIRL POWER

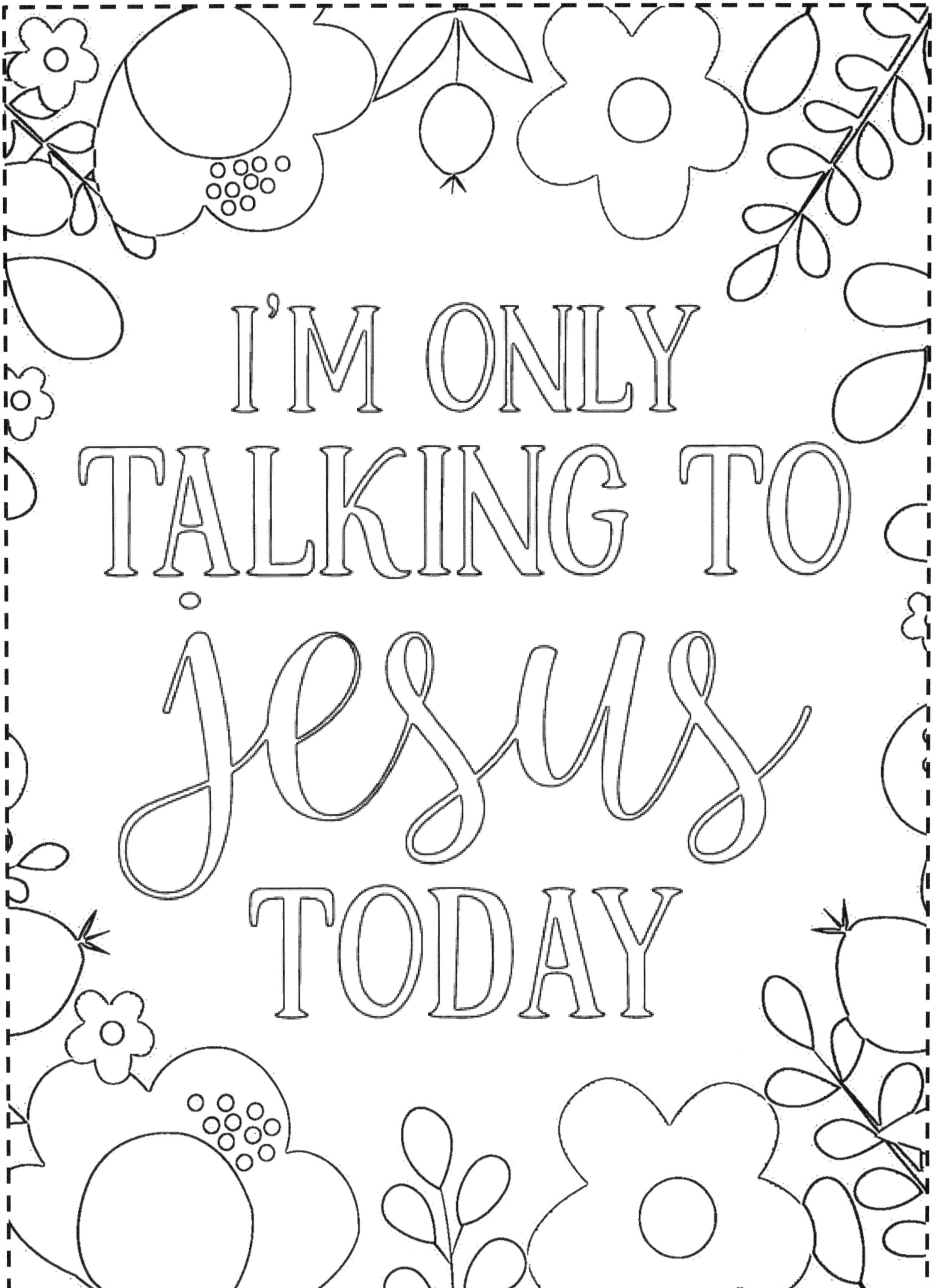
I'M ONLY
TALKING TO
Jesus
TODAY

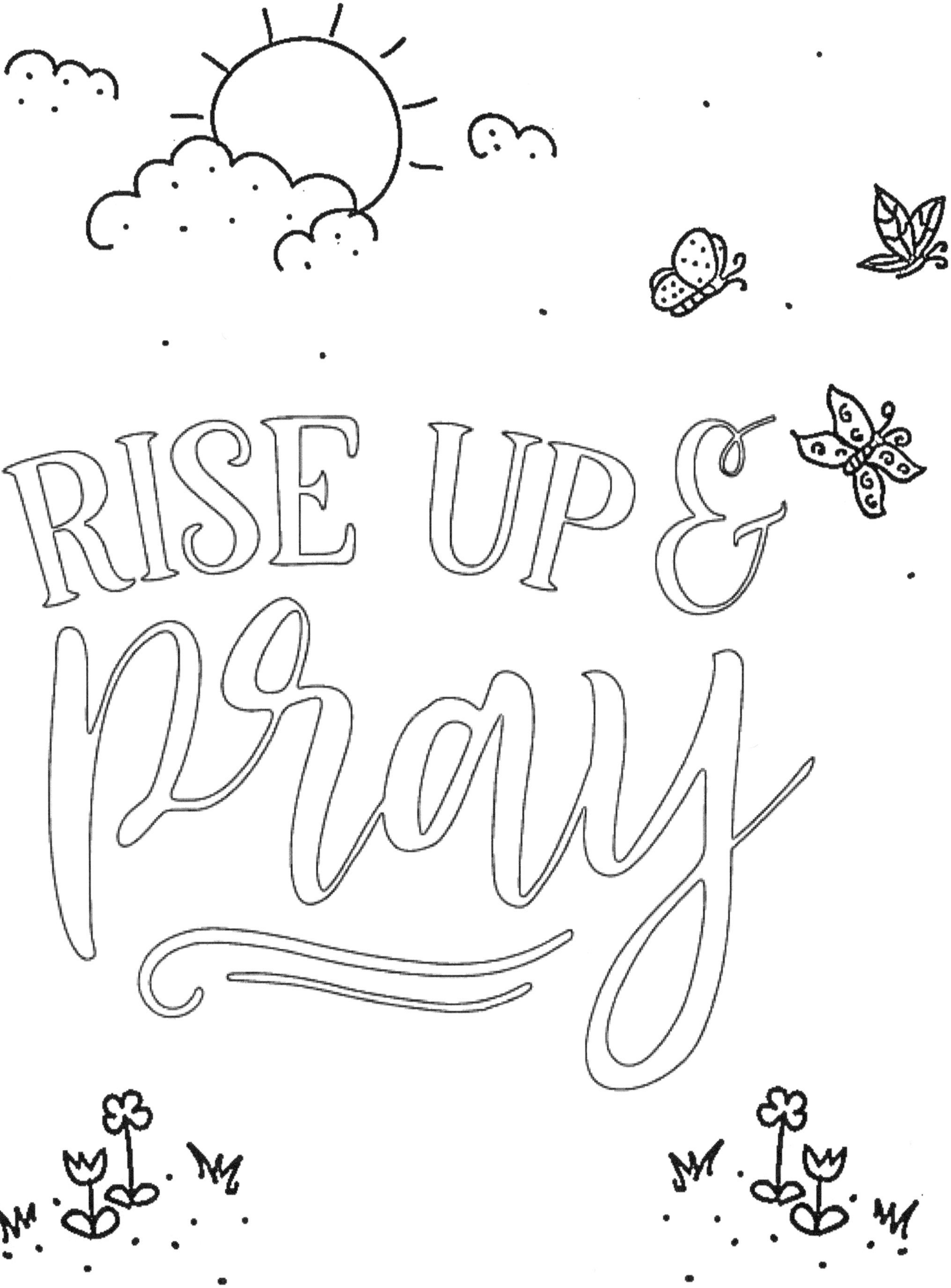
RISE UP &
pray

JESUS is essential

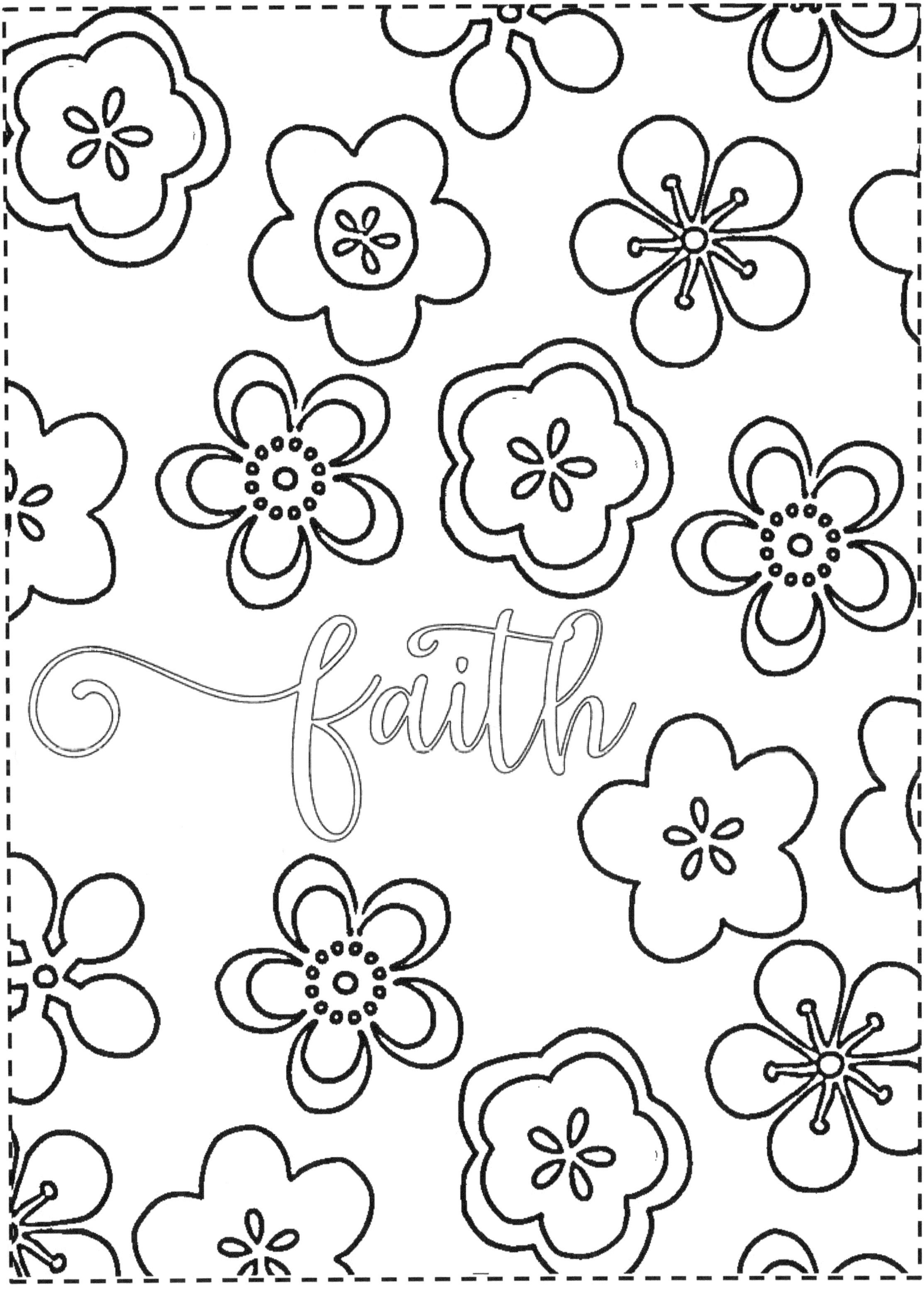
faith

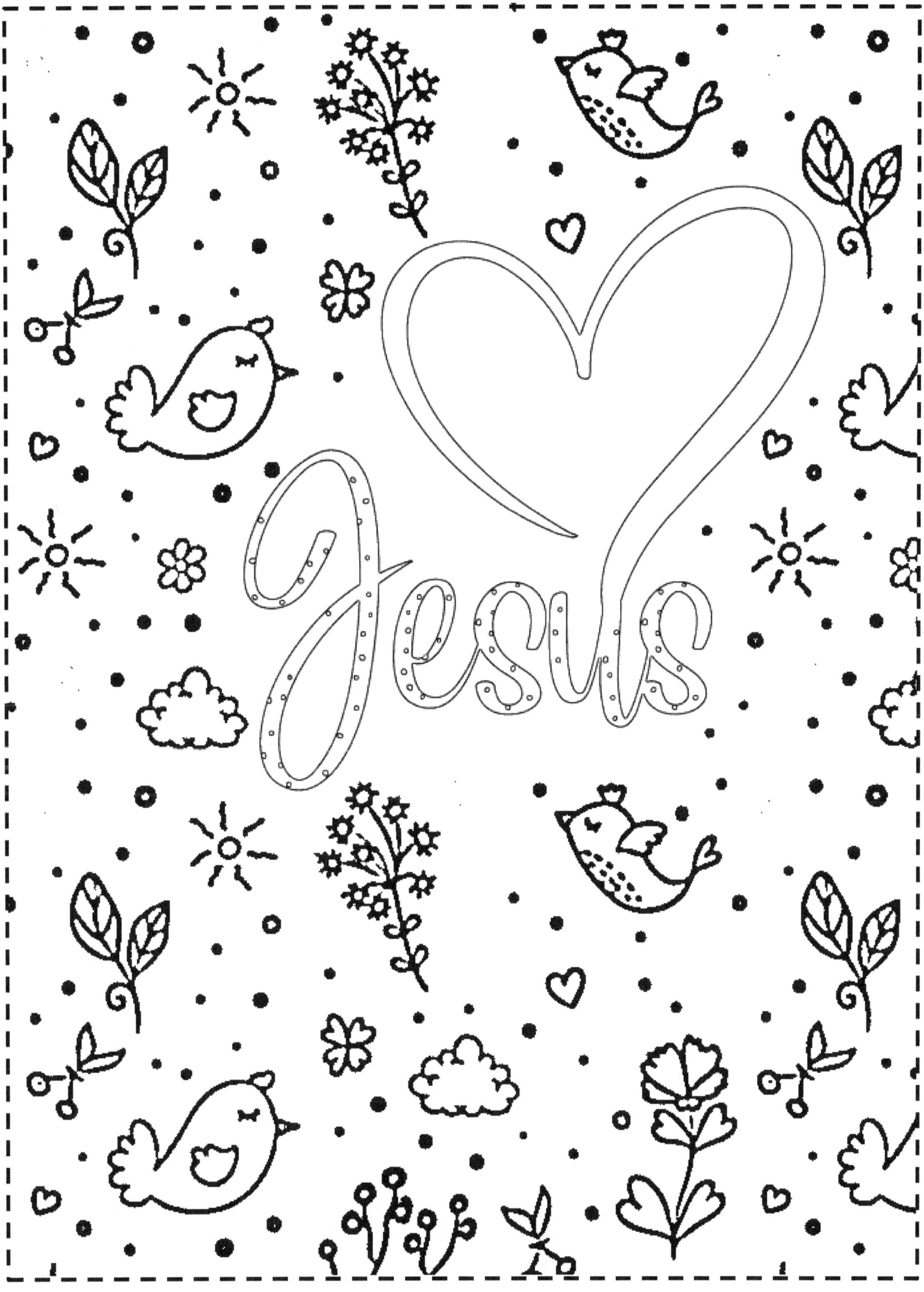
Jesus

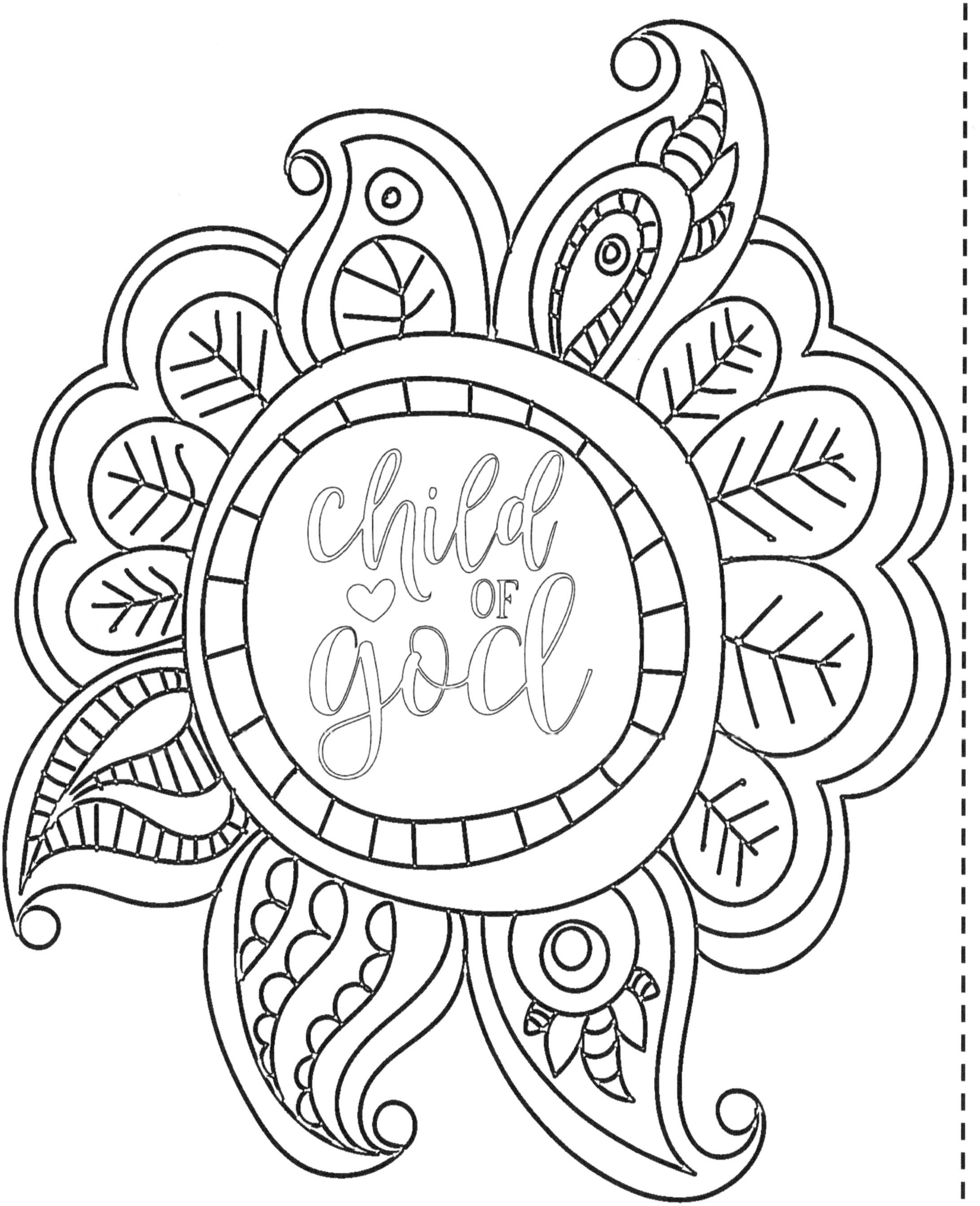
child of god

www.ingramcontent.com/pod-product-compliance
Lightning Source LLC
Chambersburg PA
CBHW081005220526
45467CB00008B/2702
9798728433842